Presents

Kerry Burton-Galley
is a writer, artist, and animal rights activist.
She lives with her husband, Nigel,
and their Thai rescue dog,
nestled between the Moors and the Dales.

What the Deserts Would Tell You

desert facts for kind and curious little minds

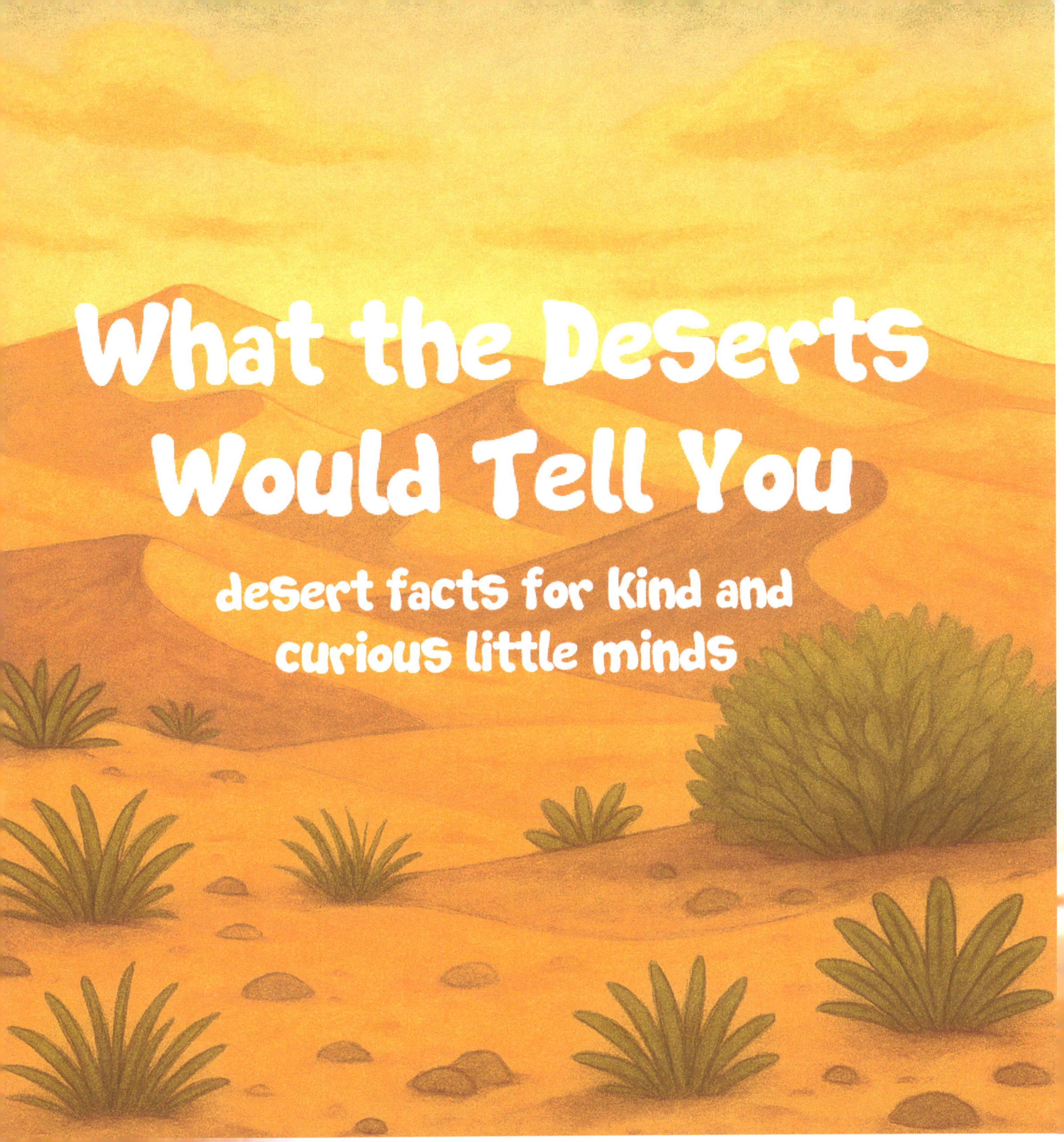

Copyright © 2025 Kerry Burton-Galley
Copyright © 3 Gargoyles Publishing
Cover image and illustrations
Copyright © Kerry Burton-Galley

The right of Kerry Burton-Galley to be identified as the author
of this work has been asserted by her in accordance
with section 77 and 78 of the Copyright,
Designs and Patents Act, 1988.
All rights reserved.

No part of this publication may be reproduced or transmitted
or utilized in any form or by any means
(electronic, mechanical, photocopying or otherwise)
without permission in writing from the publisher.

ISBN: 978-1-0684629-9-3

For the animals

FACT
Rain is Rare!
Some deserts get rain only once a year — and some might not see a single drop for many years! When rain finally does fall, it can turn the whole landscape into a burst of colour!

FACT
Camels Are Built for the Desert!

Camels can go days without water, using the fat in their humps for energy. But that's not all — they can also close their nostrils to keep out blowing sand during desert storms!

FACT
Cactus Spines Protect Their Water!
Cactus spines are there for a reason — they stop thirsty animals from biting into them and stealing the water stored inside. They also give the cactus a little shade to help keep cool in the blazing sun!

FACT

Vultures Have a Weird Way to Cool Down!

To stay cool in the heat, vultures pee on their own legs! It might sound gross, but it really helps lower their body temperature.

FACT
Many Desert Animals Are Pale!

Many desert animals are light-coloured to help them stay cool. That's because darker colours soak up more heat from the sun, but pale colours reflect it. It also helps smaller animals and insects blend into the sand and stay hidden.

FACT
Not All Deserts Are Hot

When you think of deserts, you might picture a fiery sun and sand dunes — but Antarctica is actually the coldest desert on Earth! It's not the heat that makes a desert, but how little rain it gets. Even snow-covered places can be deserts.

PROBLEM
We're Getting Too Many Deserts!

When people farm animals like cows and sheep, the animals eat all the plants and squash the soil with their feet. Some farms also use too much water or plant the same crops over and over again. This all makes the soil hard and tired — and then nothing can grow, making more deserts. And while deserts are interesting, having too many is harmful to the planet.

WHAT CAN WE DO TO HELP?
Make Good Choices!

When we care for the land, it stays healthy —
for animals, plants, and people too.
Being vegan doesn't just help animals — it also
saves water, protects plants, and helps stop
more deserts developing.

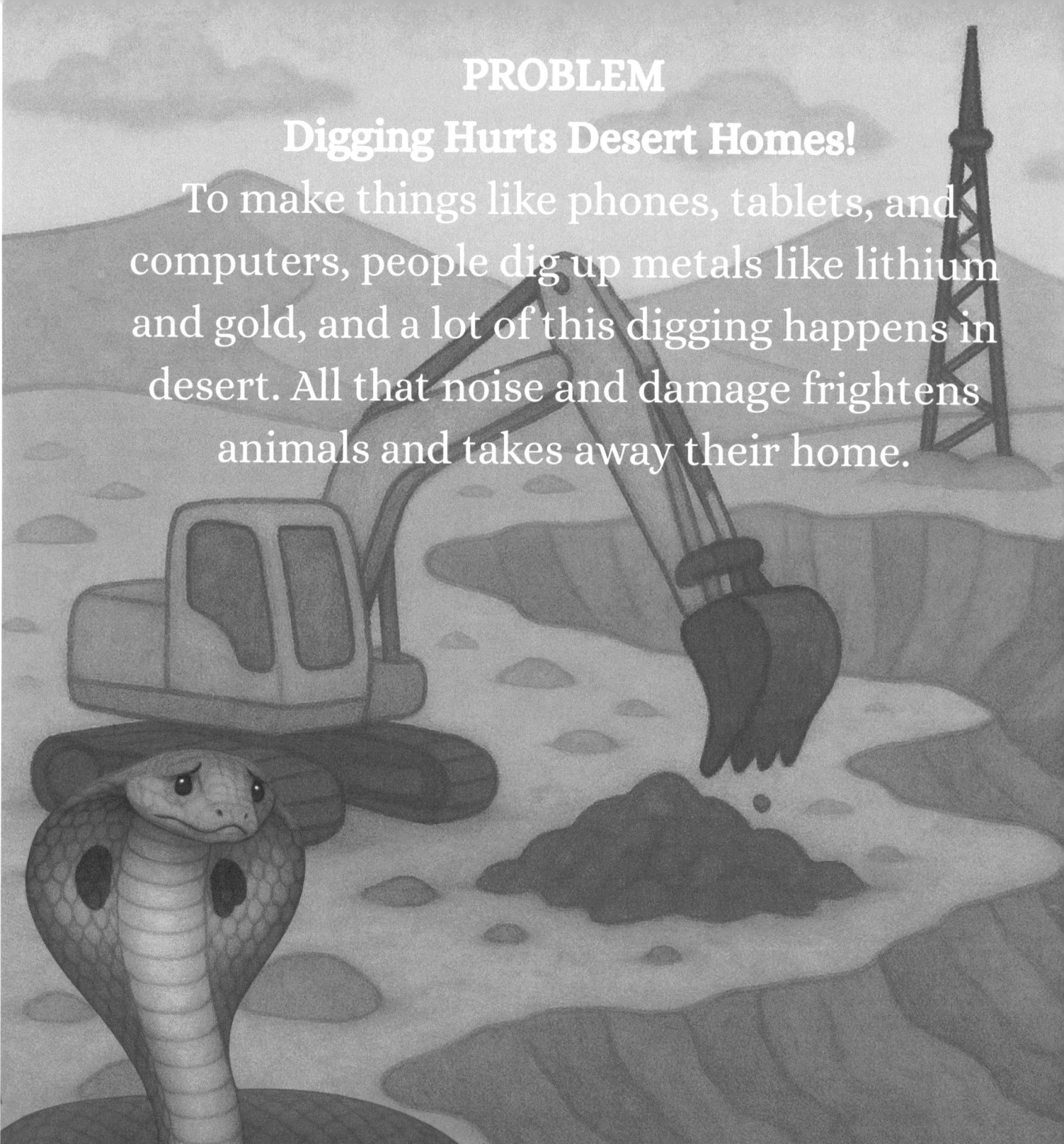

PROBLEM
Digging Hurts Desert Homes!

To make things like phones, tablets, and computers, people dig up metals like lithium and gold, and a lot of this digging happens in desert. All that noise and damage frightens animals and takes away their home.

HOW CAN WE HELP?
Be Tech Smart!

You can help by only getting new gadgets when you really need them, passing old ones on, or taking care to recycle them properly.

PROBLEM
Deserts Are Getting Hotter!

When we burn things like oil and coal, it puts gases in the air that trap heat. This makes the planet hotter, and deserts even drier. Too much heat can make it hard for animals and plants to survive.

HOW CAN WE HELP?
Use More Green Energy!

Solar panels and wind turbines make electricity without polluting the air or harming animals. Unlike petrol or coal, green energy doesn't make the Earth hotter. By using solar power and being careful with electricity at home, we help the planet stay cool, clean, and safe for everyone.

FACT
The Sahara Has Super-Speedy Ants!

The Saharan silver ant is the fastest ant on Earth! They race across the hot sand so quickly, their little legs hardly touch the ground.

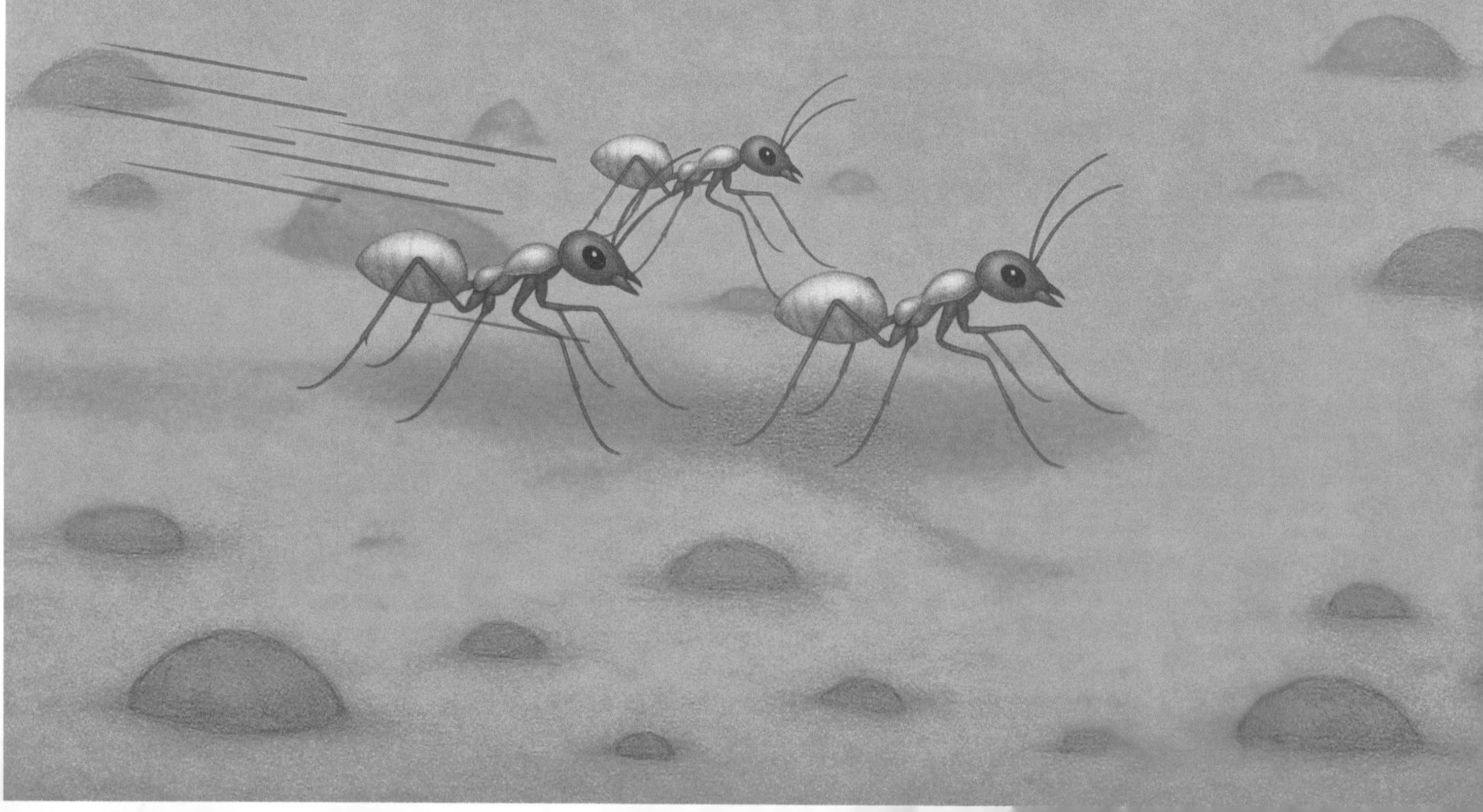

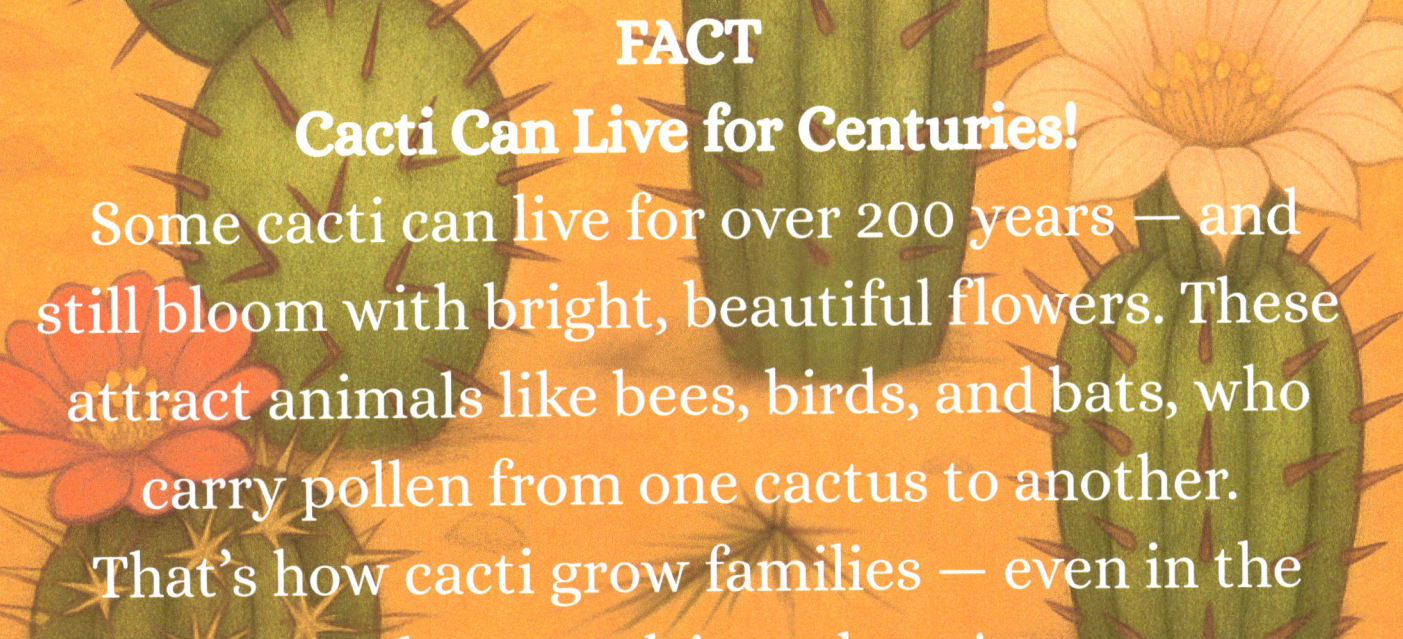

FACT
Cacti Can Live for Centuries!

Some cacti can live for over 200 years — and still bloom with bright, beautiful flowers. These attract animals like bees, birds, and bats, who carry pollen from one cactus to another. That's how cacti grow families — even in the hottest, driest places!

FACT
Desert Dirt is Alive!

It might look dry and empty, but desert soil is full of tiny living things called microbes. These tiny helpers make it possible for desert plants to grow — even in tough conditions!

FACT

Deserts Can Freeze at Night!

Deserts are boiling hot by day, but freezing at night! That's because there are hardly any clouds to trap the day's heat, so it escapes into the sky after sunset.

FACT
Big Ears Help Fennec Foxes Stay Cool!

Fennec foxes have huge ears — and they're not just for listening! While their giant ears do help them hear insects and prey underground, they also release heat to keep the fox cool in the sizzling desert sun.

FACT

Desert Dust Travels the World!

Tiny bits of desert dust don't just stay in the sand — the wind carries them across oceans to feed coral reefs and rainforests far away. Even deserts help life grow!

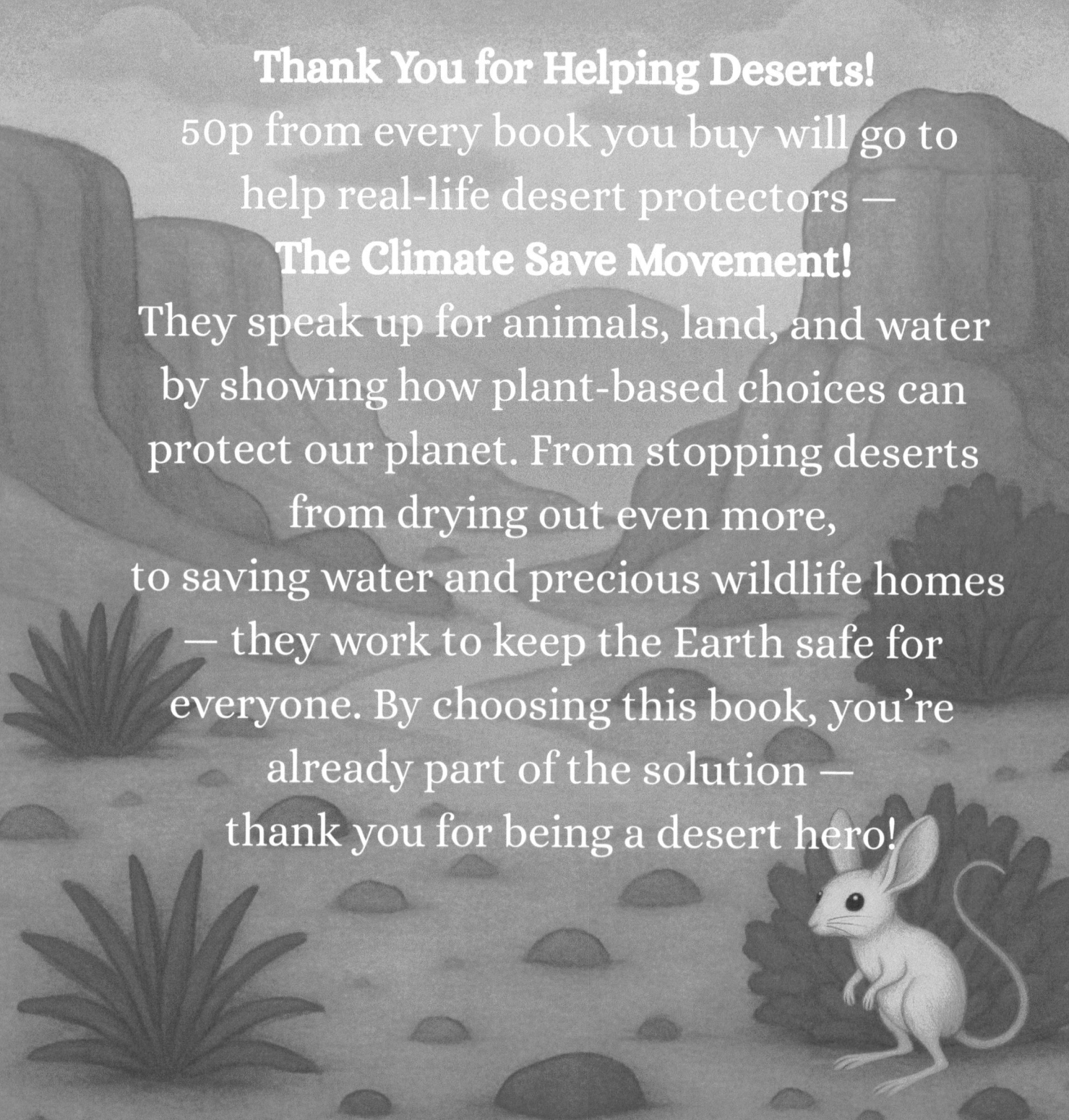

Thank You for Helping Deserts!

50p from every book you buy will go to help real-life desert protectors —
The Climate Save Movement!
They speak up for animals, land, and water by showing how plant-based choices can protect our planet. From stopping deserts from drying out even more, to saving water and precious wildlife homes — they work to keep the Earth safe for everyone. By choosing this book, you're already part of the solution — thank you for being a desert hero!

ACKNOWLEDGEMENTS

Mama — you worked through heat and heartache, so I could have a world filled with stories, wonder, and care. Thank you for showing me that even in the harshest places, life finds a way.

www.ingramcontent.com/pod-product-compliance
Lightning Source LLC
Chambersburg PA
CBHW041444010526
44119CB00043B/494